THE AMISH RESEARCH GUIDE

Crafted for the Englisher
Writer and Non-Writer

Written by D. Gan

ISBN-13: 978-0994827005

ACKNOWLEDGEMENTS

Thanks to my clients, who prompted me to learn enough about the Amish to be able to walk in their shoes and write fiction about them as if I were indeed one of them.

And thanks to my husband, who allowed me the time to write even when there were so many other "more" pressing things that needed to be done.

Table of Contents

INTRODUCTION: WHAT IS THERE ABOUT THE AMISH? 1

THE AMISH NOVEL 2

    TYPES OF AMISH FICTION 5

AN AMISH PRIMER..7

    WHAT ARE THE DIFFERENT TYPES OF AMISH?..9
    WHAT LANGUAGES DO THEY SPEAK? 11
    WHAT IS AN AMISH COMMUNITY LIKE? 11
    WHERE DO THEY LIVE? 13
    WHERE DO THEY WORK? 14
    WHAT IS THEIR FINANCIAL MANAGEMENT LIKE? 15
    TRUE SEPARATION OF CHURCH AND STATE..16

CHURCH WORSHIP, RELIGIOUS CEREMONIES AND COMMUNITY INTEGRATION
....18

    BELIEFS 18
    CHURCH LEADERSHIP POSITIONS..20
    SUNDAY CHURCH SERVICES..22
    COMMUNION AND FOOT-WASHING 24
    BAPTISM 25
    COURTING AND WEDDINGS 25
    FUNERALS..29
    HOLY DAYS 31
    SUNDAY EVENING SINGS 31
    CHURCH DISCIPLINE (THE ORDNUNG) AND EXCOMMUNICATION 32
    EVANGELISM AND NEW MEMBERS 33

FAMILY LIFE 35

    MEALS AND MENU ITEMS 37
    EDUCATION 38
    HEALTH CARE 39
    RUMSPRINGA (OR RUNNING AROUND) 40
    MARRIAGE..41
    FAMILY ENTERTAINMENT 42
    ART, HOBBIES AND CRAFTS 44
    HOME FURNISHINGS AND DECORATIONS 44

ATTIRE 45

WOMEN 45

MEN 46

CHILDREN 47

APPLIANCES, TOOLS AND EQUIPMENT 48

TECHNOLOGY IN THE HOME...48

TECHNOLOGY IN BUSINESSES AND ON THE FARM.......................................50

COMMUNICATION, GADGETS AND TRANSPORTATION.............52

TELEPHONE...52

COMPUTER 52

CAMERA..52

TRANSPORTATION 53

AMISH LANGUAGE 55

COMMON AMISH NAMES, FIRST AND LAST, FOR FICTION WRITERS.....58

CONCLUSION 60

ABOUT THE AUTHOR...62

"Wherefore come out from among them, and be ye separate, saith the Lord...." (II Corinthians 6:17)

Introduction: What Is There About the Amish?

T he Amish are a fascinating people, to be sure, but so are many other peoples around the world. Perhaps the interest in the Plain People stems from a perverse response to their strong determination to be left alone, apart from the world? Or is it because they evoke in the minds of us harried "Moderns" a quieter, simpler time, when community members actually supported each other and families spent their whole lives together, from cradle to grave? Whatever the reason, just mentioning the word *Amish* will cause tourists to tingle with excited anticipation and stonehearted book editors to take a more serious look at an unproven writer's first romance novel.

This book was written with fellow novelists in mind, and certain sections of it (such as the first chapter) are written specifically for that group, after my own journey into writing fiction about a group of people whom I needed to research extensively before I could write with confidence. But it also will be helpful to nonfiction writers, researchers and people who simply want to learn more about this intriguing group for their own enrichment.

If you have no interest in writing about the Amish but would simply like to learn more about them, skip to the Amish Primer chapter, which summarizes various aspects of the (mainly Old Order) Amish lifestyle.

Feedback regarding this book would be most appreciated and can be directed to the author at *dgailauthor@gmail.com*.

The Amish Novel

Move over vampire romances. The Amish novel is here! Sales of bonnet books, as they are often called, have been gathering steady momentum since the late 1970s, when author Beverly Lewis unleashed her Amish novel *The Shunning.*

Amish fiction, and especially romance fiction, is popular with readers and publishers alike. It is one genre of "Christian" fiction that is not exclusively sought after by Christian publishers; secular publishers are on the hunt for it, too. And freelance writers and ghostwriters are producing (hopefully) high-quality Amish novels and novellas by the volumes to meet the demand.

An Amish novel is a welcome relief for a freelancer such as me, who draws the line on creating certain types of equally popular fictional genres, including vampire romances.

What's the attraction of this line of fiction?

In the United States, the Amish make up a small percentage of the population (Old Order Amish number nearly 300,000 but are rapidly growing organically as they favor large families, and few children leave the church. According to some sources, the Amish population doubles in size every 20 years, making it one of the fastest-growing populations in the world).

The Amish (there are different types, but most fiction revolves around Old Order, or House Amish as they are sometimes called because they meet in private homes rather than meeting places) are best known for refusing modern conveniences such as electricity, which most of us find essential. Rather than drive cars, they get around town in horse-drawn buggies. Although they are concentrated in specific regions of the United States, especially in Pennsylvania, Ohio, Indiana, Delaware and New York, most of us have seen at least one horse-drawn Amish buggy meandering along on the side of a busy highway or an Amish vegetable stand stationed patiently by the road. Did we take a moment to look at them with awe?

These people are like a step back in time, to an era when farming, family and faith were central to what many perceive as being a much more satisfying existence. They have simply refused to change as the world around them has evolved. We may ask ourselves, how can they live that way? But their simpler, quieter, insulated lifestyle is attractive to us at some level. Wouldn't it be nice to be liberated from all the craziness and demands of modern life? To live a life truly dedicated to the loftier ideals of family and community, with God at the center of it all?

Therein lies the attraction of Amish fiction. They are like historical novels set in the present day. They promise a brief escape from a world of busyness, pressures, and, yes, worldly perversion and corruption. That's not to say the Amish aren't faced daily with their own set of challenges. It is developing these prickly issues in your characters' lives that will make your work irresistible to your readers.

If you write eBooks, for someone else or in your own name, for self-publishing platforms such as Smashwords or Amazon Kindle Direct Publishing, it is very likely that you are not Amish and never have been. This is a no-brainer because practicing Amish do not use personal computers or the Internet, except in rare commercial situations. You may have left the church at some point or have had close contact with an Amish community. If so, you are one of the lucky ones amongst the would-be Amish novelists. Most of us Englishers, or Moderns as we non-Amish are sometimes dubbed, have had little or no close personal contact with this elusive group.

Some will say, "Well, you shouldn't be writing about a group you have no personal experience with."

My response is, "Why not?" Do I need to experience the Civil War to write a historical novel that takes place during the Civil War, or do I need to live in Kenya to write an adventure story set in Nairobi? Absolutely not. But I do need to research until I know enough to write as well as I would if I did personally experience this time or place—or interaction with this group of people.

Have you been assigned to ghostwrite an Amish romance novel? Excited but apprehensive about this opportunity? Perhaps asking yourself, *How can I write anything genuine about these people when I don't know much about them? There are no Amish around here to visit and glean a few pointers.*

If you are like me, you will want your work to be entertaining but also as close to the facts as possible.

So, where do you begin if you are hired to write an Amish novel, or if you simply yearn to write one for your own personal edification? The plot isn't really the problem (characters are characters; they all share common problems and obstacles, no matter to what religious or atheistic belief system they adhere) as much as ensuring that you understand this group of people well enough to write from their perspective with confidence.

Small details matter. In two of my Amish novels (written in the third person but from the heroines' viewpoints), I had my heroines use an old trick to make their physical appearances come alive to readers: look at themselves in mirrors. But then I came across a reference that indicated Amish do not own mirrors, fearing they will promote vanity.

Oops! But can't mirrors also be used for practical purposes, such as maneuvering long, self-willed hair into those tight, neat buns that can be captured in an organdy prayer cap?

Luckily, an Internet search produced as many yeas as nays to the question of whether the Amish have mirrors in their homes.

If you expect a consistent answer to a question you have about their way of life, you may not find it, depending on what question you ask. The Amish have no central authority. Each district produces its own set of rules, called the Ordnung (German for order), and there are differences from district to district. Sticking to the mirror issue for a moment, some districts forbid them, but others do allow them. Next to none would permit large, showy mirrors with huge, clunky gold frames; these would be considered a vain and unnecessary display. Plain, simple, functional mirrors can be found in Amish homes. They may also be found on their buggies for help with traffic monitoring. In fact, mirrors are more accepted among the Amish than photographs, which are universally forbidden, especially facial close-ups. Although a church member might be tempted to admire his or her reflection in a mirror, the experience is not a permanent record, as a photograph is.

Do you see what the core theme is here? Humility. If a single thread needs to be interwoven into your story, it is humility, assuming your characters stay true to their Amish roots.

So there's no way around it. If you want to write an authentic Amish story, you will need to do the research. And the less personal experience you have had with the Amish, the more research will be involved. And research takes time. The more time needed for research, the longer it will take you to write your book.

This book aims to cut your research time dramatically while providing accurate, factual details that you can use in your novel.

Types of Amish fiction

The good news for those who like to write short, compact stories with zero fluff is that short fiction is popular. Short reads are perfect for the reader on the run, the reader who wants to devour a complete and satisfying story on his or her (usually her) tablet during an hour-long lunch break. The 800-page epic novel is much less popular on today's digital readers than they are in printed form, so if you are writing primarily eBooks, shorter can be better.

Short novels can be as short as 7,000-10,000 words. Much shorter than that, and readers may feel cheated, and they may demand a refund—although there is a category on Amazon for 15-minute reads that includes Amish titles that are as brief as 2,000 words. The short story is a challenge to write. In a romance story, for example, the writer must introduce a sufficient number of challenges and obstacles for the main characters to overcome and resolve by the end. No room for secondary character development here. The one and only focus will have to be on the hero and heroine, on their journey from enmity to true love.

Novellas are longer, 10,000 to 50,000 words, giving the author more legroom to build a cast of characters, insert those beloved descriptions, weave a roller-coaster suspenseful plot. And the hurried reader will not have to invest too much time to reach that crucial climax.

A standard novel averages 75,000 words (60,000-90,000 is the norm), but the sky's the limit. If you want to write a 1,000,000-word saga, go for it. You might be wise, however, to divide it into a few separate novels, each complete with a satisfying ending that oh so subtly (or not so subtly) leads into the next. Series are popular. In fact, a common sales-boosting strategy on book-selling sites such as Amazon Kindle Direct Publishing is to offer the first novel in a series for free for a short period, hoping to improve sales (and garner those all-important reviews) for the other paid books in the series. This works especially well when all the titles in the series are available simultaneously, though the writer/publisher can promote future books through pre-orders.

Amish fiction, as with other fiction, is written in various genres, with a few exceptions. Romance is popular, but historical, mystery and suspense, Western, contemporary, young adult, children's are valid options. Just stay away from erotica, aliens and vampires if you want your work to have an authentic ring, although some writers are daring to release horror and paranormal Amish fiction. However, if you are writing an eBook that becomes a hit and later goes to print, or if you self-publish your work in printed form alongside the eBook version using print-on-demand printers such as KDP Print, Lightning Source or IngramSpark, your print book can be marketed to the Amish (many of whom are avid readers—hey, without modern conveniences such as television, Netflix, DVD rentals, what's one of their main forms of entertainment?). You don't want to hide your head in shame when they reveal your work to be fraudulent in reflecting their way of life. So let's move on to that crucial research part.

An Amish Primer

"Apart...but together."

From where did the Amish originate?

The Amish feel a close connection to martyrdom, and rightly so, if you look at their history. The Amish, along with the Mennonites and Brethren, originate from Swiss Anabaptists. They gained traction during the 16th century Protestant Reformation era. Anabaptist is short for re-baptizers, those who re-baptize adult believers who were previously baptized as infants. Back in the mid-millennium of 1000-2000 AD, infant baptism was the accepted Christian practice.

They are also known for their "two kingdoms" doctrine, which stresses the importance of its adherents living separately from the world, because a devout Christian cannot serve two masters (Jesus Christ and the world). Anabaptists emphasize serving Christ first. They strongly advocate for the separation of church and state, a very unpopular viewpoint during the Reformation period in Europe that earned them some powerful enemies in high places. They view themselves as following Scripture literally.

Today's Amish are descendants of the close followers of Jakobb Ammann (1644-1720?), a Swiss Brethren/Mennonite leader who in 1693 began to lead his group to split from the main body of Anabaptists (primarily Mennonites), whom Ammann felt were too liberal by not closely following the teachings of the Mennonite founder, the converted Dutch Catholic priest Menno Simons, and the Dordrecht Confession of Faith (1632), a Dutch Mennonite statement of faith containing 18 articles that outline their religious beliefs.

You will find when studying the Amish that the issue of shunning, using the threat of social exclusion to strongly encourage church members to obey the rules (not Biblical rules necessarily but those agreed upon by their communities in their own tailor-made, unwritten Ordnungs, which do vary from district to district), is a fundamental theme throughout Amish history until the present day. Disagreements over this thorny issue have resulted in Amish splitting from Mennonites, Amish splitting from Amish, Amish individuals leaving or being forced out of the Amish church. It was primarily because Jakobb Ammann felt the Mennonites were too soft on shunning excommunicated members that the Amish came to be.

And shunning has provided innumerable storylines for Amish fiction writers.

Is there any Biblical basis for shunning? On the surface, it seems cruel and heartless. The main verses used to justify shunning are Paul's I Corinthians 5:11-13, arguably the most controversial in the Bible: "But now I have written unto you not to keep company, if any man that is called a brother be a fornicator, or covetous, or an idolater, or a railer, or a drunkard, or an extortioner; with such an one no not to eat. For what have I to do to judge them also that are without? Do not ye judge them that are within? But them that are without God judgeth. Therefore put away from among yourselves that wicked person."

These are strong words, and shunning is a strong practice. Used in the right way, though, shunning is meant to work for the victim's benefit. The hope is that he or she will repent, turn from his or her ungodly ways, confess publicly and return to the fold. If shunning is used in a cruel and smug manner, then the "shunner" is sinning against the "shunned" and ultimately God.

The Amish began immigrating to North America in the 18th century, in large measure because of religious persecution (Catholics and Protestants alike in the Old World considered their Anabaptist teachings subversive and viewed them as heretics) and to avoid military service. They met in private homes to worship as meeting in designated buildings of worship was too dangerous, a custom that is still practiced by Old Order Amish today. There are no Amish remaining in Europe. Those who stayed in Europe were absorbed into other Anabaptist groups, primarily Mennonite. Their hymnal, the *Ausbund* (German for paragon), highlights the martyrdom theme through its somewhat somber songs that are without musical notations. Their sense of martyrdom has contributed toward fostering their strong desire to stay separate from the world. Their *Martyr's Mirror* book chronicles their history, emphasizing honoring those who died for their faith.

The Amish settled first in Berks County, Pennsylvania, due to Quaker William Penn's "holy experiment" of religious tolerance and subsequently spread out into the rest of the country, most recently setting up settlements in Western states such as Colorado and Montana. Lancaster County, Pennsylvania, is considered one of their oldest and most expansive settlement districts and is today a hot spot for Amish-hunting tourists.

History and the past still dominate the Amish lifestyle, lending that peculiar attraction that is so compelling to some Englishers. They seem intent on maintaining the way of life they brought to these shores in the 18th century, and they do a remarkable job of it, even as the rest of the world lunges into the future at an ever-quickening pace.

What are the different types of Amish?

There are several different Amish splinter groups, spawned mainly by Ordnung-related disputes, but these are the main ones.

The Old Order Amish are the group we tend to think of first when we think of Amish, but they actually sit in the middle on the conservative/liberal scale. In the United States, they broke away from the main body of Amish Mennonites in the mid-1800s over doctrinal disputes, preferring a more conservative, traditional lifestyle, and new, more or less conservative groups have broken away from them over the years. The Amish Mennonites are today known as Mennonites. For the fiction writer, the assumption will be that your characters are of the Old Order group, unless otherwise stated.

Overall, the Amish are a patriarchal society, with older men wielding the most clout, younger women commanding the least. There is a pecking order in the Amish community, with church leaders reporting to God, men in the congregation taking their lead, women following their husbands, and children obeying their parents. They value the tried and true and are slow to change with the times. When changes are made, they are agreed upon by the community after being first discussed at length by the church leaders. There are no quick decisions with the Amish.

The Swartzentruber are more conservative than the Old Order Amish but fewer in number. They splintered off from the Old Order Amish in 1913 because they regarded the latter as being too modern. You can only imagine how strict they are. They do not recognize other Amish faiths as truly Christian and do not permit intermarrying with other Amish groups. Their Ordnungs are restrictive to the extreme, governing every aspect of their lives, and they speak strictly German at home. Children learn English only at school.

The Andy Weaver Amish are a conservative offshoot of the Old Order, and they are centered in Holmes County, Ohio, where they arose in the 1950s in response to an issue revolving around shunning. They lie somewhere in between the Swartzentruber and Old Order on the strictness meter. They are a small group comprising about 40 church districts. They speak Pennsylvania German at home.

The New Order Amish are more (but less in some respects) liberal than the Old Order. In the 1960s, they split with the Old Order Amish. The former accept more technological innovations, especially farm machinery, and social changes than the Old Order but are stricter regarding tobacco and alcohol use as well as courting practices. Many districts hold Sunday services in church houses.

The Beachy Amish Mennonites are the most liberal of all, arising in Pennsylvania in the 1920s after dividing from an Old Order district. In many ways, they are closer to Mennonites than Amish and are characterized by their greater commitment to mission work.

What languages do they speak?

At home, most Old Order Amish speak a combination of Pennsylvania Dutch (which is a German dialect) and English. Pennsylvania Dutch differs significantly from the official German language. Parts of church services are conducted in High German, other parts in Pennsylvania Dutch. Children are usually not taught English until shortly before they attend school at age 6. Parents try to immerse them in Pennsylvania Dutch at an early age so that they will regard it as their official language. When communicating with non-Amish, Amish are fluent in English and will revert to Pennsylvania Dutch only in the presence of an Englisher when speaking with their young children (or if they want to tell another Amish adult something they don't want the Englisher to understand!).

Some expressions that we consider polite, such as "please" and "thank you", are not used much by the Amish, who consider them unnecessary. Later on in this book, we will look at a few Pennsylvania Dutch words and phrases.

What is an Amish community like?

The Amish are truly communitarian rather than individualistic. The welfare of the community as a whole dominates over that of its individual citizens. Individual members cannot live just as they please. They must always be cognizant of the rules and regulations put in place by the community. In exchange for sacrificing self-volition, each member receives whatever support and help he or she needs. This mindset is epitomized by the famous barn-raising, wherein the community rallies around the victims to clean up the debris and raise the new, better and stronger barn in a day. If an Amish family moves into a new home, they will not need to hire a moving company; dozens of fellow church members will lend a hand. Their separation from the world intensifies their dependence on each other.

The German word *gelassenheit* is synonymous with submission and self-surrender, primarily to God's will but also to the Amish community. It is the antithesis of self-interest and individualism. Members are to use their skills and energies not for self-promotion but community-promotion and to do so with that all-important humility. If a church member misses the message on the importance of being humble, he or she may be labeled as being proud in the area of his or her weakness. For example, "horse proud" if he or she takes great pride in his or her beautiful buggy stallion, "Scripture proud" if he or she shows off by reciting Scripture.

Close-knit does not even begin to describe the typical Amish community. Knocking on a neighbor's door is one practice that simply doesn't happen. An Amish home is always open to another Amish, so long as they are in good standing with the church (i.e., not excommunicated). A visitor can walk in without any kind of announcement at any time. If he or she arrives right before a meal, that individual will almost be guaranteed an invitation to join in. Visiting is a popular recreation in itself, occurring more in the fall and early winter after the harvest, when farm chores slow down. Frolics are organized events to help church members in need and are well attended by all.

Women and older girls participate in gatherings tailor-made for them, such as quilting bees or getting together for "sisters' days" to produce pies, preserved jams or chow chow pickle relish.

As individuals and communities, they do not follow the principles of self-achievement that guide most Americans, and, in fact, those principles that are taught as fundamental. If they seem disconnected from the society around them, it is because they are.

Americans are to be independent, to make the most of themselves; Amish are to be self-effacing, to work hard for the good of family and community. Americans should be proud of their accomplishments; Amish should remain modest and shun self-gratification. Americans should strive to be number one; Amish are content to live quietly and behind the scenes in this world, knowing that the true rewards and glory come later, in Heaven. Americans emphasize finding self; Amish emphasize losing self.

Where do they live?

Most Amish live in rural communities. The ideal is for each baptized man to own his own farm to cultivate with his wife's and children's help. Farming brings the Amish closer to God's creation and fulfills God's original assignment to Adam and Eve to be earth's caretakers, to till the ground. The ideal Amish farm size is 40 acres, which is considered a manageable size for a horse or mule to maintain. Despite the emphasis on farming, some Amish have moved to more urban settings, working for non-Amish "Englisher" factories or operating their own businesses. Amish are famous for making quality furniture and sheds. Amish women are known far and wide for their lovely quilts. Despite their humility, they believe in producing products that are worth every penny paid for them and more.

Today, they live in several states, approximately 30, with the majority of settlements in Amish strongholds in Pennsylvania, Ohio, Illinois, Iowa, Indiana and New York. Settlements are geographic clusters of districts. Some settlements may include only one district. Affiliations are groups of districts that are united by similar beliefs and practices.

Districts are the building blocks of Amish communities, made up of 20 to at the very most 50 families. There is no central Amish authority. Amish districts are guided by their own version of the Ordnung, an unwritten set of rules that each baptized church member vows to follow and passes down to the next generation. The Ordnung is reviewed twice a year at congregational meetings and can be changed if church members agree. Often, there will be a discussion about how new technologies might be introduced or adapted and the impact of adoption on the community. Districts are limited by how many people can congregate in a private home for biweekly church services (Old Order Amish do not have dedicated church buildings). As Amish families average seven children, 35 families would mean 245 people packing into one home on a Sunday morning. That's a lot of people!

The critical need for affordable farmland by a rapidly expanding Amish population has prompted many to move west, establishing settlements in Kansas, Minnesota, Missouri, Montana. There are more than two dozen affiliations, 500 settlements and 2,000 self-governing districts nationwide. The largest concentration is in Holmes, Ohio. There are also Amish pockets in the Canadian province of Ontario. Interestingly, more than half of the population is under the age of 18.

As a rule, Amish get along well with their non-Amish neighbors, who view them as ideal neighbors, though horse manure on public roads and sidewalks has been a prickly issue in some communities!

Where do they work?

The Amish's top choice for employment is farming. This has been their mainstay occupation for centuries. It perfectly encapsulates their values of hard work, long hours, family members laboring side by side, being God's relentless caretakers on earth. But the high price of farmland in their traditional areas of the country, such as Pennsylvania and Ohio, has forced some of them to move west (where farmland is much less expensive) or seek employment in factories or with construction companies, usually owned and operated by non-Amish, taking them away from home and into the danger zone. Even when employed by Moderns, though, they stick to tradition by, for example, hanging onto their straw hats rather than wearing standard safety headgear, causing their employers to weigh the options of adhering to safety regulations or employing strong, reliable, honest workers.

Operating a small cottage industry is a popular alternative to farming; the husband may open a woodworking manufacturing or machinery repair shop, sell books or dry goods or leather products from a small store, or operate a greenhouse or sawmill; the wife may help out with a quilt, craft, jam or bakery shop. This allows them to stay close to home and enlist the help of their children, which furthers their practical education. Some Amish are carpenters by trade, making furniture, cabinets, sheds, lawn furniture that has earned a reputation worldwide for quality and durability.

Another option is to work in trades: plumbing, electrical, heating, carpentry, roofing. This will take them away from home part of the day, but they can usually work locally. And it will spare them from having to work in a non-Amish factory, which will likely require a fair commute away from home.

Some Amish stick with standard time the year through and do not observe daylight savings time, which can be a hurdle for those employed by non-Amish.

What is their financial management like?

Amish use ordinary local banks for business and personal finances; need I write that banking is done in the branch, not online?

It is universally true that the husband is responsible for managing the family's finances, except in rare circumstances. The Amish are known for their frugality, viewing their resources as belonging to God, with themselves as mere managers. They save money on everyday needs by growing their own food and making their own clothing.

Credit-card use is limited to Amish businesses. They prefer cash or bartering.

The Amish love a good deal and will attend auction sales. Sometimes being the successful bidder involves a competitive spirit, which is uncharacteristic of them.

Their basic expenses tend to be much less than the average North American's: no cable TV, no electricity, no Internet, no insurance, no credit-card interest, much less in gas payments (gas is used not in vehicles but to power equipment such as generators), likely no Bell phone (unless they share a phone shanty with neighbors). Their horse feed costs are more, though!

After graduating from school, young teens help their parents with farm or house work, depending on their sex, but may also work outside the home. Boys may work as apprentices in trades, girls in restaurants as waitresses or private homes as house cleaners. Their earnings will probably be given to their parents for household expenses, as they are still living in the home, but the parents may set aside a percentage as a savings account for the child.

True separation of church and state

The Amish respect governing authorities but avoid contact with them as much as possible. They minimize their dependence on the government by building up their communities. They do not receive social assistance or government payments of any kind, relying on their communities for help as needed. They do not accept insurance payments, public or private. If a community member needs expensive and extensive medical care, not to worry. His or her community will come to his or her aid. Most communities have a special fund to support their members in need. If the funds are depleted, the bishop and/or deacon will solicit church members to add contributions.

They do pay income (federal and state) taxes, estate taxes, property taxes but are officially exempt from paying Social Security and Medicare taxes, as they do not receive Social Security benefits. They must provide proof that they are Amish to the appropriate authorities to receive this exemption.

The Amish do not relish conflicts and will go out of their way to avoid getting into a debate or fight. They are recognized for their stance as conscientious objectors, opposing any personal involvement in national conflicts. They refuse to fight in wars and are exempt from active military duty. They take Jesus's teachings regarding turning the other cheek literally. They determine to surrender their rights to take revenge when they suffer harm from another person. Their pacifist stance has not made them popular with some other citizens of the United States, who feel every American has the duty and responsibility to take up arms if required to do so to defend his or her country or national interests overseas. In general, they go to great lengths to avoid confrontation in court and outside of it.

They are unable to swear an oath in court and instead make affirmations of truth. Many but not all refuse to vote in federal and state elections. They will not hold public offices. Most will not pledge allegiance to the flag, nor will Amish school teachers ask students to pledge allegiance to the flag in class.

If a crime is committed within the Amish community, church leaders prefer to settle it themselves, if at all possible, without involving the state authorities. Sometimes they cannot help but get the authorities involved, such as if they suffer harassment from non-Amish. Serious incidences of violence against Amish are rare today, but non-Amish troublemakers still pelt buggies with objects, especially at night.

Amish are not encouraged to join broader non-Amish organizations or service clubs, but many volunteer for the fire department.

Church Worship, Religious Ceremonies and Community Integration

"Pure religion and undefiled before God and the Father is this...to keep himself unspotted from the world." (James 1:27)

One feature that makes the Amish unique is how their lives revolve around their interpretation of the Christian faith. Their faith is central to their lifestyles. They live by values they believe are necessary to please God. Many of the qualities we Westerners hold dear are anathema to the Amish, such as individual achievement. They stress qualities many Americans consider "wimpy," such as modesty and purity. Humility rather than pride, simple pleasures rather than extravagance, separate from rather than joined to the pollutions of the world—these principles guide their churches as well as their homes. They live as part of a tight-knit, faith-based community, independent from the world but dependent on each other.

To other Christians, they may seem unusually detached from the world. They view themselves as pilgrims passing through to a better place, their real home. As such, they aim not to develop a significant emotional attachment to this world.

There are few out in the world, luckily a small few, who find this determined detachment despicable.

Beliefs

Many of the Amish theological beliefs are common with other Christian denominations. They are sometimes identified as Calvinists, believing in God's ultimate sovereignty. Whatever He has determined to happen will happen, no matter what we humans do. They will look for His signs to determine His will for the course of action they should take. They particularly stress the importance of believer's baptism—adult baptism of those who truly believe the Gospel of Jesus Christ as opposed to infant baptism of those who are too young to have a clue. Amish baptism involves not only a commitment to follow Jesus but a lifelong commitment to the Amish church and obedience to the rules of the community's Ordnung. Submission to the authority of the church is fundamental.

The triune godhead, virgin birth, bodily believer resurrection, Heaven and Hell, grace from God through faith in Jesus are tenets shared with many other denominations. The Amish stress favorite sections of the Bible, such as the Sermon on the Mount (Matthew 5-7). Although the Bible is their blueprint for everyday living, they do not encourage personal Bible study achievement, lest the individual boastfully displays his or her superior knowledge.

For the Amish, though, salvation through the grace (an unearned, undeserved gift) that Jesus offers is supplemented with the concept of working out one's salvation daily through righteous living. Some Amish will say that salvation comes by obedience, not grace. And obedience to God comes through obedience to the church's rules, even more so than individual interpretation of Scripture. They do not believe that a Christian is guaranteed salvation based on faith in Jesus Christ alone, considering this belief in the assurance of salvation to be prideful. A follower of Christ must put godly principles into action. And even then, salvation is not sure but a "blessed hope". Amish, like other Christians, see themselves as ideally being transformed into the image of Christ. Granting salvation is very much at the discretion of God on an individual basis. And if a member "sins" and leaves the church, they are virtually guaranteed a spot in Hell should they remain unrepentant, even if they join a different Christian church, according to many Amish.

They may see the role of the Christian not so much to win the lost but show them by example how to live a holy life, uninfluenced by the world, pure and unstained from the shenanigans of the devil. Like the Old Testament Jews, they emphasize the importance of separating themselves from the temptation to sin by not mixing with the "heathen".

Amish will, and rightly so, point to the failings of many Christians who are quick to receive the gift of salvation through faith in Jesus Christ but slow to put Biblical teachings to work in their lifestyles, as if believing that "anything goes" for the Christian, who is guaranteed his or her place in Heaven no matter how he or she lives.

Evangelicals will argue that the Amish works philosophy diminishes the sacrifice Jesus made on the cross, which is all-sufficient to cover our sins and gain our entry into Heaven, at least for those of us who believe in Him and accept His sacrifice to pay our sin debt. Like the Old Testament Jews, the Amish attempt to be holy in their own right by obeying their own laws, an impossible feat.

Who's right? That may be a question to be fully answered in Heaven.

Some Amish believe that their church has received authority from God to set the acceptable standards to live by in today's society. Other Christians will accuse them of trying to add new laws to the Bible, which they claim is a complete representation of God's will for all believers. The Amish see their Christian faith as dictating a holy lifestyle. They do not deny that Jesus, the Son of God, is the only way to peace with God, but they add to His free gift the necessity to do good works and "live holy". Reaching Heaven is the end game, and hope is in the reward God has set aside for those whose good works outnumber their bad.

A few Amish are on the superstitious side. Don't ask an Amish woman to pick up a dropped sewing needle between Christmas and New Year, for example. Some keep their female animals away from the slaughtering outbuilding on a farm, as they fear any close contact could be an invitation to a miscarriage.

Amish are admirable for walking the talk, while too many other Christians simply talk the talk. Their beliefs are evident in the way they live their lives. It's not easy to live a good Amish life. That is why the support of their friends and family is so invaluable.

Church leadership positions

The Amish church is founded on lay leadership. The Amish do not subscribe to formal religious education. Only baptized men can hold leadership positions in an Amish church. These are unpaid positions that last for life. They are often called "servants" to stress the congregation's emphasis on humility. Bishops are known as servants with full powers, ministers as servants of the book and deacons as servants to the poor. New deacons and ministers (at least two at a time per district) are chosen by a combination of vote and lot from among the baptized men in the congregation following a biannual communion service. Candidates are made candidates when they receive three or more votes from other members, then each selects a hymnal. The ones who find Scripture verses inside their hymnals win the seats. The Amish feel God selects His own ministers through this process.

The bishop, the highest office in the church, is chosen from the serving ministers. His appointment must be approved by the congregation and the other bishops in the settlement. He provides spiritual leadership and presides over important services, such as baptisms, communions, weddings, funerals, ordinations and excommunications. He interprets the Ordnung for the congregation and evaluates any suggested changes, looking for ways in which they may negatively impact the community. If he feels these changes will harm the community spiritually, he will block them, as his mandate is to safeguard Amish traditions. He may serve two districts simultaneously.

Most churches have two or three ministers, who assist the bishop with preaching. They preach long, somewhat spontaneous sermons. Many wear slightly wider brimmed hats than the other men in the congregation.

The deacon also participates in church services, often reading Scripture passages and leading prayers. And he administers funds to those who need help. He may assist with church discipline.

Bishops, ministers and deacons are needed not only to fill the shoes of recently deceased leaders but also to equip new districts, usually offshoots of ones that have grown too large to manage with home-based worship services. When a church district grows so that the members can no longer fit inside a private home or barn, it splits off and creates a new church district with its own set of church leaders, and its own Ordnung, of course.

Sunday church services

Sunday morning church services are the pinnacle of the Amish two-week cycle. They are long by most standards, on average three hours, starting at 8:30 and ending at 11:30, followed by lunch. Some districts hold even longer services. They are held in private homes on a rotating basis every other Sunday morning. While each district holds a service every two weeks, individual members may attend the services of other districts on their off-service Sunday mornings, if they can squeeze in! They transport backless benches using a bench wagon from house to house before the services. This practice of holding services in homes was passed down from the church's earliest founders and may have its roots in the persecution Anabaptists faced in Europe, making home services relatively safe. It also limits each district's size, as the necessity to cram all church members into a house or barn for worship sets an upper limit on the number of members a district can accommodate.

Seating arrangements follow the established pattern of the community. For example, married men may sit at the front. Young unmarried women behind them. Married women and their young children in the dining room and kitchen. Generally, young children sit with their mothers, but youth sit in gender-specific sections.

Services comprise singing songs by memory from the *Ausbund* hymnal without the accompaniment of musical instruments, prayer, Scripture readings in High German, at least a couple of sermons that may be in Pennsylvania Dutch, followed by commentary on the sermons from baptized men. The *Ausbund*, written in German and dating back to the 16th century, is a compilation of verses written by martyrs and other Anabaptists sung to long, slow, monotone German folk tunes and chants that have been passed down through the years. Newer hymns have been added to the core hymns written by the original 53 incarcerated writers, and some recent editions of the *Ausbund* contain hundreds of pages. It is said to be one of the oldest Protestant hymnals still used. Male song leaders help the congregation render the songs, sometimes lasting a quarter of an hour just for a few stanzas. "Das Loblied" is a hymn of praise that is a favorite and traditionally the second hymn sung during an Amish service.

There are at least two sermons. The first is shorter, about 30 minutes in length, followed later by the longer sermon, lasting an hour or more. Sermons are usually given in Pennsylvania Dutch, and the leaders choose who will give them at the start of each service. Ministers may give sermons in a sing-song manner.

Sunday service provides an opportunity for members to confess their sins, especially if they have broken the Ordnung, and ask forgiveness. This usually prevents them from being put under the Bann, excommunicated then shunned, whereby the other community members go out of their way to have no direct contact with them.

There is no Sunday school, except in some New Order Amish churches.

After the service, benches are transformed into tables for a light lunch, called Liebesmahl, the "love" meal. Because of the crowd, attendees usually eat in shifts in separate rooms; men and children often eat first as the women are busy with the preparations. Church spread, a peanut butter and marshmallow combination on bread, is a popular menu item. But the meal may include any variety of food items, everything from meats and cheeses to homemade apple butter and pickles. Snitz, a pie made from dried apple slices, is likely to cap the menu. The Amish are in no hurry to return home. After everyone has finally eaten, a social time follows.

Church attendees tend to socialize with people of their own age and sex after services.

On non-church Sundays, members are expected to visit family and neighbors or attend other districts' church services, space permitting.

Communion and foot-washing

Communion is the most important service for the Amish as a group, stressing the importance of connecting with God, spiritual revival, self-examination. The eight-hour service is held twice a year, in the spring and fall. Everyone partakes in a meal together as well as the remembrance of Christ's sacrifice with bread and wine. Communion services are preceded by council meetings, or Members Meetings, during which members resolve any differences so that each church member can partake in communion with a clean heart (or as close to clean as is humanly possible). The congregation examines their Ordnung and considers any proposals for revisions, carefully considering how they would affect the community if implemented. If someone pushes too vehemently for change, he or she may be labeled a "fence jumper". The church's leadership meets before the congregational meeting to discuss how new innovations should be handled before bringing the issues to the church as a whole for a vote. Those who feel led confess their sins before God and fellow church members. This meeting is considered crucially important as a way to cleanse the church in preparation for communion.

Foot-washing is a practice taken right out of the New Testament (John 13:14: "If I then, your Lord and Master, have washed your feet, ye also ought to wash one another's feet") and again emphasizes the importance of humility, of putting others before ourselves. Pairs wash each other's feet.

Offerings are taken during the communion services and passed onto the deacon to help the needy, the only times collections are taken. Because there are no church maintenance costs or pastors' salaries to cover, the funds are used strictly for charity.

For the Amish, communion is a twice-a-year opportunity to reconfirm their allegiance to God and their church/community (i.e., each other).

Baptism

Adult believer baptism is central to the Amish faith. It is a commitment not just to God through faith in Christ but to the local Amish church. They do not baptize infants. Most candidates are between the ages of 17 and 22 when receiving baptism. Baptismal services usually occur in the spring. Adult baptisms are accomplished through sprinkling on the head (three times) rather than full immersion. Candidates will have completed 12 to 18 weeks of baptismal classes with the bishops, ministers and deacons conducted on each church Sunday. These classes involve reviewing the 18 articles of the Dordrecht Confession in German (with the goal of being able to recite them in German at the end). And also the district's Ordnung. Baptismal candidates may be voted in to receive baptism by the congregation after a period of demonstrating how "righteously" they can live.

The bishop leads the baptismal service, which may follow one of a variety of formats outlined in their prayer book. The service itself usually ends with a "holy kiss", from the bishop to male candidates, his wife to female. After his or her baptism, the baptized becomes a full voting member of the church and also subject to the rules of the church's Ordnung, to which he or she vowed obedience during the baptismal service. Disobedience can and does lead to excommunication, or the Bann, and shunning (severing social ties with the individual).

Newly baptized men are immediately eligible to be enlisted as a deacon or minister sometime in the future.

Courting and weddings

Baptized Amish marry other baptized church members (**both must be baptized**) in a private home, usually the home of the bride's parents. In some communities, a blue gate signifies that a girl eligible to be married lives there. Courting customarily begins when the young people are between 16 to 18 years of age, though girls may be as young as 14. Boys must be at least 16, though, or they will likely be teased for jumping the gun. Courting is common during Rumspringa, a "running around" period during which young people are allowed by some communities to experience the ways of the world to make an informed choice.

Sunday night sings, on church service Sundays and held in the house or barn of the family that earlier held the church service, are great opportunities for boy to meet girl. These are often well attended, with young people from other districts flocking in. Typically, the boys will sit on one side of a long table (if the house is so equipped), and the girls on the other. They sing until 10 PM or so, with lots of socialization between songs and for a couple of hours afterward. The boy typically invites the girl (or asks a friend to ask her for him) to ride with him back to her home in his two-seater courting buggy. Dating couples spend evenings chatting in the girl's home; they may go out to eat together and attend other community functions, or just sit in the courting buggy and chat and drink hot chocolate and sodas. Generally, they keep their relationship fairly private. At this point in their lives, they are not yet baptized, so they are free from the regulations of the district's Ordnung, though still subject to their parents' guidelines.

Some Old Order Amish permit a practice called bundling, or bed courtship, where the two young people lie side by side on the girl's bed and chat—fully clothed, of course. But interestingly, New Order Amish have banned the practice, as it has proved to introduce too much temptation to sexual proximity in some instances. Living together before marriage is not permitted by any of the Amish. Occasionally a wedding is hurriedly arranged due to unplanned pregnancy and may occur any time of the year. The young mother-to-be must often confess her indiscretion in front of the church, should she want to stay in good standing with the church and be baptized. A problem arises when the father of the unborn baby does not want to marry the girl. Abortion is not an option, so the pregnant girl may be married off to an older

Amish widower in some cases. That way, she can still be part of the church after she is baptized.

Courtships can last awhile, three to four years. It is unusual for a young man or woman not to be married by their mid-20s, but most marry after they reach the age of 21. The husband-to-be gives his fiancée a gift when he proposes. They will ask their parents for their approval to marry. In mid-October, shortly after the semi-annual communion service, their plans to marry are announced, or published, in front of the congregation at the end of a Sunday morning service. The deacon reads their names. In some communities, the bride and groom do not attend this service but instead stay at the bride's home socializing.

Because of the small gene pool, there are rules on how close the couple can be in terms of bloodlines. Second cousins are permitted to marry, but not first.

Joy-filled parents may be seen planting lots of celery over the course of the summer. Celery is an Amish wedding staple. Celery is used in the Amish casserole (chicken and stuffing) and creamed celery for the wedding day meal, but its main use is decoration on the tables, especially the tables of the youth invited.

Weddings are huge events for the Amish. The proud groom is generally elected to go around the community personally inviting guests. Weddings usually occur after the fall harvest, from late October through December; November is the most popular month. With weddings all being scheduled within the same time frame, it can be very busy for the community.

Hundreds of guests may descend on the house of the host (almost always the bride's family or friends of the bride's family), which will have been made spotless over the previous weeks. If the bride's parents ever needed help from their community, it is now, for their beloved daughter's wedding. Unbelievably in some Amish communities, neither the parents of the bride nor the parents of the groom attend the actual ceremony. They usually assign one female organizer to oversee the cooks, servers, dishwashers. Men are needed to keep the horses and buggies outside under control; they enlist the help of teen boys, called hostlers.

Weddings are usually held on Tuesdays or Thursdays so that there is time to prepare for and then clean up after them. No guest need be in a hurry on wedding day! The actual ceremony follows a two-to-three-hour morning church service, which is similar to the Sunday service. The lucky males in the wedding party, side sitters, lead the females in, and they sit on backless benches facing each other while the hours-long wedding service and ceremony get underway. The bride and groom enter the scene while everyone is singing "Das Loblied". They hold hands during the ceremony, the first and last time in public. Men in the congregation remove their hats to show respect for the God-ordained aspect of the ceremony. More than the usual number of ministers may be in attendance, as many as 12. Similar to Englisher ceremonies, a minister will ask the bride and groom questions (often privately in a separate room) before giving them his blessing. The new bride will be directed to be submissive to her new husband.

Then comes a hearty noon meal (the first of two meals), featuring the roast, Amish casserole, mashed potatoes, coleslaw, thick gooey apple sauce and that creamed celery. Because of space limitations, food prep is usually accomplished in an outbuilding and rushed in. Or the ceremony may be in the house of friends of the bride, the cooking and meal in the bride's house. The Amish do not shun desserts, which include pies and donuts and puddings, as well as several wedding cakes, which are usually consumed later in the day.

In many cases, noon meals are served on the seating benches, and guests must eat in shifts because of the sheer number of them. The bride and groom, along with the bridesmaids and groomsmen they have chosen to be in their wedding party, receive seats of honor. They will have earned their meal because they will have been busy earlier greeting guests as they arrive. Ushers and waiters, usually four married couples, seat guests according to certain criteria, such as age, sex, relationship to bride and groom. After they eat, guests enjoy an afternoon of singing, games and socializing. Then another meal in the evening (lighter with warmed-over leftovers from the noon meal plus extras such as baked oysters and lemon pie), more games and more singing. Finally, around 10:30, the exhausted bride and groom are allowed to begin their new life together.

The bride may be dressed in white (if so, she may well be buried in this dress later on), but a new pale blue linen dress is the usual choice. She will wear no makeup or jewelry, and she will not receive a wedding ring, as wearing jewelry is forbidden by almost every Ordnung. Her dress will be plain with no frills such as lace. She won't wear a veil but instead her white prayer cap and apron (this may be the first time she has worn a white prayer cap as many unmarried Amish women wear black caps and aprons). The prayer cap and apron that she wears will be saved for her funeral, but she may wear her wedding dress again to special occasions.

The groom (previously clean-shaven) will have already started growing his beard and will actually wear something Amish men normally do not wear, a tie (a bow tie, as will his groomsmen). His shoes will be black, high top. After the ceremony, the groom may undergo a traditional rite of passage ceremony, whereby he is passed over a fence by a group of unmarried men to a group of married men.

The newlyweds spend their first night together in the bride's home. But they don't have intercourse right away, sometimes not until their fourth night of marriage. Their first full day of being man and wife will be consumed with the cleanup. They will live at the bride's home over the winter and visit friends and relatives over the next few weeks, basically everyone who attended their wedding, gradually receiving all of their wedding gifts. In time they will move into their own house, usually in the spring. The husband will be well on his way to sporting that trademark Amish beard.

Funerals

Funerals are a sad time for the Amish, as they are with all people. But the Amish make less of them than adherents of many other religions, possibly because of their strong hope that the deceased is now in a better place. Customs differ from district to district and according to state regulations. In some communities, the body is taken to a local funeral director, preferably one who has experience with Amish funeral customs. The body is embalmed if required by state law and often covered in white underwear. The plain casket is usually delivered to the closest relatives' home and placed in the house or the barn. Family members will then further dress the body in white, sometimes a white shroud, covered with a white sheet. A woman is sometimes dressed in her wedding dress, if it is white, or a long white dress. The white cap and apron she wore on her wedding day will be arranged on the body, again highlighting the importance of this pivotal day in her life. A man may be dressed in a white shirt, vest, pants. No makeup will be applied to the corpse. The casket will be appropriately simple with no adornments, made of local pine.

Although the community will know about the death shortly after it occurs, the family often places a short obituary in the local newspaper. Usually, two to three days after the death and the day prior to the funeral service, friends and neighbors come to view the body. Most guests are Amish, but English friends are welcome, too, if they had a relationship with the deceased.

The room in which the casket sits will not have any other furniture in it. There will be viewings at the home, then finally at the gravesite. The first part of the funeral service is conducted right in the home but may then be moved to a barn, if there is more space. Guests do wear black. Amish homes are not typically decorated with flowers for funerals.

The Amish treat their deceased with humility. They do not publicly extol his or her personal virtues. There is no eulogy. Instead, the bishop or minister will give a sermon in Pennsylvania Dutch, referring to Scripture teachings about creation or the resurrection. The first ceremony, in the house, is usually approximately 20 minutes. Then a longer service is held, possibly out in the barn to accommodate all of the guests, who can be numerous, reaching into the mid-hundreds. This service, too, is highlighted with teachings about God and prayers, with very little said about the deceased. There is no singing; hymns are spoken.

Women may hang their bonnets and capes on the clothesline outside to signify the event.

After the casket is carried out headfirst, it is positioned in a horse-drawn enclosed hearse wagon (if the district has one). Unless the family has its own burial plot, the solemn procession of buggies to the cemetery is an arresting sight for those who witness it. The deceased is buried facing east, so he or she will be ready for resurrection day. Family members may throw clumps of sod onto the casket once it has been lowered in the ground by ropes. The grave is dug on the spot by men of the community equipped with shovels. Wooden tomb markers are plain and uniform, sometimes giving only the deceased's first name but usually supplying the individual's full name, dates of birth and death, possibly his or her age, usually in English but sometimes in German. Children may be buried in unmarked graves. The community may keep a map showing the location of each grave.

Usually, the bishop but sometimes a minister reads a hymn, and the attendees pray the Lord's Prayer silently. Some guests will go back to the house for a small meal, which is much less elaborate than the wedding meal and served rather informally. The family will enter into a mourning period, and friends and family will visit them on off-service Sundays for up to a year.

Holy days

The Amish celebrate the same holy days as the rest of the Christian church: Thanksgiving, Christmas, Easter, Ascension Day, Pentecost being the main ones. Some have a fast day on October 11. Small Christmas gifts are exchanged, but Amish contain their excitement, and the practice is not commercialized, as it is in today's Western culture. Some Old Order groups celebrate

Christmas on January 6, calling it der Alt Grischtdaag, or Old Christmas.

Sunday evening sings

Twice a month, on church service Sundays, large groups (as many as 150) of young people in their late teens, some from other districts, gather in the house in which the morning worship service was held for Sunday night sings. These get-togethers are social times, and courting among the unhitched is encouraged. The goal, of course, is to produce a few fall weddings. Participants play games such as volleyball and baseball, enjoy a light meal, all of which is followed by several hours of singing from their *Unparteiische Liedersammlung* hymnal, a shorter hymnal with faster tunes than the historical *Ausbund*. Boys, dressed in their gut (good) courting clothes and looking as neat as possible, will have arrived in their courting buggies with their sisters or friends of their sisters' but never their actual girlfriends. Instead, boys invite girls (maedels) for a ride home in their courting buggies, and socializing may continue for a few more hours at the girls' houses.

Church discipline (the Ordnung) and excommunication

During baptism, church members vow to uphold the requirements of their district's Ordnung, a verbal set of rules that is agreed upon by local church members. These rules have a purpose; they are meant to help the congregation lead godly lives by providing a code of behavior. They reflect the Amish love for old traditions and suspicion toward change. Anyone caught breaking one of those codes will be disciplined, even to the point of excommunication and ostracization (shunning, or meidung). This cutting off from the relationships that Amish value so highly is emotionally painful—and can be economically painful if the individual depends on the support of other Amish for his or her business endeavors. There is Biblical support for the practice: I Corinthians 5:11 ("But now I have written unto you not to keep company, if any man that is called a brother be a fornicator, or covetous, or an idolater, or a railer, or a drunkard, or an extortioner; with such an one no not to eat") and Romans 16: 17 ("Now I beseech you, brethren, mark them which cause divisions and offences contrary to the doctrine which ye have learned; and avoid them").

Shunning is a very effective way to enforce the rules of the Ordnung through social exclusion. The purity of the church comes first. There is no room in the Amish church for apostates. But shunning is a progressive process, with many attempts of steadily increasing severity to prompt the "rebel" to conform to church requirements. Excommunication requires a congregational vote following the recommendation of church leaders. Shunning is excommunication put into practice through social isolation of the offender, until such a time as he or she acknowledges the error of his or her ways and repents.

So shunning need not be permanent. The hope is that it will cause the offender to repent and return to the fold. If the church member does turn back, he or she will normally be forgiven and accepted back into church fellowship.

Remember that only baptized church members are disciplined. Amish who have grown up in the community but have decided against baptism are free to live outside of the rules of their community's Ordnung. They will not be excommunicated for breaking them because they have not vowed to follow them. Even so, most in the church will regard them as lost, as on their way to Hell, not Heaven. Parents, in particular, will pray and hope that their children will return to the Amish church before it is too late. Many will leave their places at the table set in anticipation.

In summary, vowing to obey the Ordnung is part of the baptismal process, a part of committing one's life to the church as an active member. It is a vow that the Amish take very seriously.

Evangelism and new members

The Amish church grows virtually completely from within. It is difficult for non-Amish to join. He or she must pass a "proving" to ensure he or she possesses the requisite strong and steadfast faith. And because a baptized Amish man or woman is allowed to marry only another baptized Amish church member, bringing a non-Amish into the community simply through marriage doesn't work.

Old Order Amish are not known for their evangelism or missionary efforts, though some New Order members are much more proactive in this area. This is one of the main complaints lodged against them by other Christians. They excel at demonstrating how to live a separated life, untarnished by the world's influences and temptations. As a rule, they do not seek to make new disciples among the unchurched or other Christian denominations. They grow because of their propensity to have large families and the high retention rate of their young. Evangelical Christians will condemn this lack of concern for the salvation of the lost sheep as contrary to the Great Commission, which calls for believers to go into all the world and make disciples of all nations (Matthew 28:19).

Family Life

F amily is central to the Amish way of life, perhaps even more so than church. Amish infants grow up in their Amish family feeling loved and cherished. Once of age, most start their own Amish families close to home, socializing throughout their lifetimes with siblings and cousins, aunts and uncles, parents and grandparents. They grow old and live with their Amish offspring. Then they pass on to what they hope is eternal life with most of their Amish loved ones in Heaven. These strong family ties provide a sense of security and belonging that is appealing to all of us, so different from the individualism of today's society that tends to cut people off into independent, self-contained worlds of their own making. Many of us yearn for a return to that tight-knit family lifestyle.

The Amish family unit is patriarchal. The husband is the undisputed head of the household. The Amish believe this role has been given to him by God and is therefore not open to debate. Women are not regarded as inferior, but their role is subordinate to that of men. Wives live under the authority of their husbands, unmarried women under their fathers'.

If you are writing fiction, you may want your heroine to be strong and independent by nature, not exactly welcoming male domination. This is perfectly permissible. Your Amish characters should seem genuine, and not every Amish woman will welcome submitting to a man. Her struggles with this necessity (if she is to remain in good standing with the church) may add some interest to your story.

Old is highly valued, and Amish elderly are often consulted by younger Amish. Old takes precedence over young, such as when waiting to be served for a meal. After retirement, the elderly generally live with one of their children rather than enter a seniors' facility. They may reside in the house, if it is large, or in a detached house (grossdaadi haus) on the property on which they raised their family. Often the farm is passed on not to the eldest but youngest son and his family once the parents are ready to retire. There is no set time for retirement. It is very much at the discretion of the individuals involved. It can occur any time between the ages of 50 and 70. Seniors will continue to help out on the farm or around the house as they are able.

The Amish wife will be a true "Jill of all trades". Her husband may be the head, but she is the undisputed manager. She will coordinate child-rearing, meals, cleaning, laundry, sewing, gardening, food preservation. She may help supplement the family income by making crafts, such as quilts, to sell. Then, when she isn't really busy, she will help her husband with farm chores.

The Amish are known for being thrifty. Waste is not part of their vocabulary. They are masters of making use of whatever they have on hand to accomplish a desired task rather than purchasing something new, such as using potato and baking powder to brighten silver and a salt solution to remove grease stains from clothing.

Baptism of both husband and wife is a prerequisite to marriage. Divorce is forbidden. Widowers, however, can and are encouraged to remarry after an appropriate period of mourning, usually two years. In unusual cases, separation may be permitted after discussion with the bishop and ministers, but the unhappy couple must stay married if they are to remain part of the church.

Children are viewed as a gift from God, the more, the better (and there is more than a slight bias toward boys). On average, Amish families boast seven children. When a child chooses not to join the Amish church but instead live as an Englisher or Modern (as 10 to 20 percent do), his or her family will be deeply hurt and disappointed. Their beloved child has gone "English". Although the individual is not shunned if he or she chooses not to be baptized, visits from him or her may not be encouraged as these can be emotionally painful for family members. Some families leave the wayward child's place at the table set in the hopes that one day he or she will decide to return to the Amish faith and be baptized.

The situation is much worse for an individual who has been baptized, vowed to be faithful to the church and subsequently leaves. This results in excommunication and shunning. The individual may leave of his or her own volition, or be forced out because of a stubborn insistence to break the Ordnung on one or more points.

Married men are eligible for church leadership positions, such as bishop, minister or deacon.

Meals and menu items

Amish eat pretty much what all the rest of us eat. They may start eating earlier, though, than the average North American family. Often the family is up at 5 AM to begin their day. Family devotions precede a hearty breakfast. They may be slower to start eating than the average family as they wait for everyone to be seated and for the head of the household to issue the prayer. But they have a reputation for being fast eaters once they get started. Usually, morning farm chores wait, then off to school for the little ones.

They grow as much of their own food as possible. As a rule, their food is not heavily seasoned, but they do add apple cider vinegar to casserole dishes. Some colorful menu items you could insert in your novel to give it a homey country Amish feel are Sweet Onion Salad, Sawdust Pie, Snitz and Knepp, Peppered Meatballs in Milk, Crybaby Cookies, Cracklings, Whole Wheat Pudding, Ham Hocks Stew, Amish Friendship Bread, Baked Oatmeal, Shoofly Pie, Tears on My Pillow Pie, Amish Funnel Cake...these are just a few. And don't forget the Dandelion Wine, which has no alcohol content but is considered medicinal. The Amish are known for their communal sweet tooth. When it comes to beverages, coffee is a favorite, but many Amish, old and young, enjoy carbonated beverages. Women wash their veggies well when cooking because they do use chemical pesticides and fertilizers on their crops.

Several good Amish cookbooks are available in print and online that will give you more menu ideas.

The kitchen makes a great setting for Amish novel scenes as Amish women spend so much time in that particular room of the house. Baking bread, preserving jams and jellies, making noodles, shelling peas and washing and cutting carrots from the garden are regular Amish women's and older girls' activities.

Education

"To fear God and to love work" is the first lesson Amish children will be taught through word and example. And it will be taught in their homes. They don't start school until they are six years old.

Most Amish children are enrolled in Amish-run, church-funded, often one-room schoolhouses from grades one through eight (from approximately the ages of 6 to 14). Schoolhouses are usually one-story with white-painted wooden siding. The teacher's desk will be made of 100 percent wood and may be quite large, stationed in front of an imposing blackboard. There may be a big cast-iron woodstove in one corner as well as several gas lanterns attached to the walls.

School ends with the eighth grade for the Amish teen. Although they are called scholars, the goal is not to produce career scholars, but productive Amish citizens equipped to work for their families within the community while also functioning as necessary in the world.

Some Amish do need to pursue higher education to be licensed to practice, such as those employed in medical and veterinary fields.

In 1972, the US Supreme Court ruled that Amish children could not be forced to continue with high school, compulsory for other American teens. Education is ongoing at home. Throughout their childhood years, children learn practical skills, such as how to operate a farm or develop homemaking skills.

On average, 30 to 50 children are taught in an Amish school at a time, and they live within walking distance of the school. Lessons are conducted in English and German and include reading, writing, spelling, penmanship, geography, history, math. The curriculum is conservative; McGuffey Readers, Dick and Jane are favorites. Only a few publishers can meet Amish standards for educational material, such as Pathway Publishers in Ontario, Canada. Bible reading, hymn singing and reciting the Lord's Prayer are also included in the daily school program, but teaching does not involve religious education.

Children are taught by single Amish women who have completed apprenticeships with experienced teachers and been approved by their local Amish school boards based on their strengths as teachers and church members. They are true multi-taskers, moving between grades throughout the day. *Blackboard Bulletin* is a publication targeted for Amish school teachers.

School hours are usually from 8:30 AM until 3:30 PM (allowing children to help out back at the farm with evening chores), and two recesses along with a lunch period break up the day. Children play games together while they are not in class or help their teacher with practical concerns, such as loading the woodstove with wood in the winter.

A few Amish mothers home-school their children.

Health care

Because Amish seem cultish to some, there are many rumors, most false, about what they do and do not do. If needed, they seek medical treatment in the same established medical clinics and facilities as any other North American. The difference is in health insurance, which they do not carry—public or private—so any funds needed to finance that treatment will be supplied by the community. They are more likely than the mainstream public to use traditional and natural remedies to heal physical problems than prescribed medications. Natural home childbirths with midwives at the helm are the norm. Their Ordnungs will give direction on how much non-Amish medical care they can receive.

Although they do not carry public health insurance, their community may require each family to contribute premiums to a community health insurance fund. They may hold special benefit auctions if a member needs to pay exorbitant health-related bills.

A common piece of misinformation regarding the Amish is that they refuse vaccinations for their children. This is not true, though they may allow them to be vaccinated less frequently.

Because of their limited gene pool (although it is prohibited for first cousins to marry, second and third cousins often do), there is a high relative incidence of genetic deformities, metabolic disorders and other chronic health conditions among the Amish. Those affected have been glad and grateful to receive assistance from researchers and other experts in the field of genetic diseases. Muscular dystrophy and dwarfism are some of the diseases that tend to have a higher incidence amongst the Amish relative to the rest of the population.

Among the conservative group, tobacco use is common, but less so with the more liberal communities, which consider smoking a health risk.

If a church member begins missing services, the congregation will become alarmed, wondering about his or her health. In general, missing three consecutive church services can be considered an offense serious enough for excommunication, but grave health issues will turn consternation into concern.

Some Amish resort to faith healers, who will perform ceremonies around the patient that may have occultist overtones to mainstream Christians. A few may be superstitious and may resort to folk remedies, such as using mare urine to treat a sore throat or skunk fat oil to relieve aching joints!

Rumspringa (or running around)

At the age of 16, many Amish youngsters are cut loose to enjoy the pleasures of the world. Because they have not yet been baptized, they have not committed themselves to follow the strict rules of their Ordnung. The expectation is that each one will, after a few months, make a firm, informed decision of whether to stay in the community and be baptized or leave it and join the world.

Most do decide to stay (between 80 and 90 percent) and be baptized, which is why the Amish population is growing so rapidly from within.

Some young people buy second-hand junkers, participate in drinking and drug binges, attend rock concerts, wear Englisher clothing such as jeans and tees. A few find themselves in hot water, but most decide to stay in their Amish communities after sampling this way of life, not wanting to forsake their close faith-based communities for the temporary "thrills" of the world. And the majority keep their Rumspringa activities relatively tame, knowing that if they decide to commit to the Amish church, they will have to confess before the congregation what they were up to during Rumspringa before being baptized. They also quickly realize that with only an 8th-grade education, they are somewhat disadvantaged in a competitive dog-eat-dog world, so different from the supportive community environment in which they have been raised. And if they leave, they will leave alone, without family support or the ties they have cherished all their lives.

Rumspringa is a very decisive time in the lives of Amish teens. The decisions they make will shape the rest of their lives.

Marriage

Rumspringa is a prime time for courting, and once old enough, many young people are baptized in the spring and marry in the fall. Although to be part of the church, two baptized church members must marry, they may be from different districts. In many ways, this is preferred as it addresses the problem of familial intermarrying, the source of several genetic diseases.

The young couple will generally live with the bride's parents until the spring, often contributing whatever income they are earning to the household fund. They may move to another district, especially in search of farmland at reasonable prices. In recent years, more Amish have been moving west to find land bargains. Usually, their parents will help them purchase a farm or start a business. If they are unable to, the community will often chip in to give the young couple that extra helping hand as they start their lives together. Some Amish businessmen are in a position to offer mortgage financing.

Family entertainment

Amish forego modern conveniences and technology in large part to avoid any distractions from family time. Space permitting, a few generations may live under one roof, or at least on the same property in separate houses. By not embracing work-saving innovations, the family works longer and harder together, building closer ties.

Televisions, radios and DVD players are not allowed, so what do the Amish primarily do for entertainment? They prefer recreation that can be enjoyed close to home and close to God's creation.

Reading books is a popular pastime, though many Amish prefer to read nonfiction, claiming that Amish fiction (written by Englisher's like us) inaccurately portrays their way of life (this book is meant to address that concern). The head of the household may read Scripture to the family in the living room in the evening. *Die Ernsthafte Christenpflicht* (The Prayer Book for Earnest Christians) is a 1700s German prayer book commonly seen in Amish homes. Prayer books may highlight the Dordrecht Confession (the Dutch Anabaptist manifesto adopted in 1632 that outlines 18 principal articles of faith), Anabaptist hymns, the order of services for baptisms and marriages, a few suggested guidelines for godly living. *Martyrs Mirror*, published in Dutch in 1660 then translated to German and English, is more than 1,500 pages long; it documents the persecutions endured by Anabaptists in 17th century Europe and is a fixture in most Amish homes.

The Budget, a weekly newspaper that has been published in Ohio since 1890, is popular with both Amish and Mennonites. Pathway Publishers, headquartered in Ontario, caters to the Amish and Mennonites. *Family Life*, *Young Companion*, *The Diary*, *Die Botschaft*, *Plain Communities Business Exchange* are other Amish/Mennonite publications that are well read by the group.

Writing letters to family and friends is a popular way to use free time. On the same track, visiting relatives and friends, especially on off-service Sundays, is an anticipated activity.

Playing games together—such as baseball, softball, volleyball, barn tag, corner ball—is another regular pastime. Young Amish children may be seen jumping up and down on trampolines. Sledding, skating and ice hockey are popular in the winter. Archery is a favorite with some. Swimming is a regular activity in the summer, but most Ordnungs forbid girls and boys to swim together. Camping is popular, along with hiking and picnics.

Crafts such as quilting and embroidery are great for combining recreation with meaningful work. Women may host quilting bees and gather in friends.

Small children play with dolls, and contrary to folklore, they are not all faceless. The faces, though, are usually very basic without any frills or expression.

Ordnungs differ, with some allowing families with children to attend country fairs. But going to the local cinema is, of course, a no-no. During Rumspringa, though, many of these rules fall by the wayside for some youngsters, who are given the freedom to experience what the world has to offer.

Amish enjoy big sales and auctions, selling quilts and baked goods and furniture and whatever else people will buy as well as looking for good bargains to purchase.

Amish definitely don't travel as much as most of us, especially those with daily farming commitments, but occasionally visit tourist spots, such as museums and zoos.

Singing is very much a part of Amish recreation, but musical instrumentation is not, although a few play the harmonica or accordion. Germanic in origin, Amish tunes are of a style of their own and are known for being slow without harmony; monophonic, without meter; long, sometimes taking 15 minutes per song. During church services, congregations often sing in High German, but outside of church services, they may sing in English.

Art, hobbies and crafts

Amish women are accomplished quilters. They have great success selling their work, especially to Englisher tourists. Because of their dread of verging on prideful, Amish art is simple and ideally is to be functional, while at the same time often displaying the beauty of God's creation through vivid colors. Needlepoint, rugs, towels may have themes, but if so will most likely be nature-related.

Other hobbies for women include gardening, canning and noodle making (an ambitious project that tends to fill the whole house).

The Amish are also renowned for their exquisite and high-quality woodworking and furniture. These items may be simple in design but are made from top-notch wood and are built to last. Amish furniture, in distinctive styles such as Mission and Shaker, is sold worldwide, and each piece may be lauded for its uniqueness. Some Amish carpenters focus on outdoor furniture.

Amish art usually needs to fulfill a functional purpose to be acceptable to church leaders, although, in some communities, they may look the other way if a member is a particularly creative artist, especially if they have a gift for expressing the wonder of God's creation. They are cautious about pieces that may verge on vanity. Art that is aesthetically beautiful but in no way practical is a prickly thorn that isn't welcome in most Amish communities.

Home furnishings and decorations

The writer who loves writing elaborate descriptions will not be inspired by the inside of the Amish home. They do not decorate just for appearance's sake. Like their clothing, the interior of their homes is plain and functional. The furniture will be sturdy and well built, made of 100 percent wood. Curtains will be plain and basic, if they are in place at all, and are sometimes single curtains that run across the window's width to save on fabric. Amish houses do not, as a rule, have shutters, which are considered an unnecessary frill.

Attire

"And be ye not conformed to this world, but be ye transformed by the renewing of your mind, that ye may prove what is that good, and acceptable, and perfect, will of God." (Romans 12:2)

The Amish realize that their clothing choices reflect their belief system, so they choose to dress plainly. No one in the community is permitted to stand out from another because of sharp and stylish clothing. The plainness of their clothing makes them stand out from the world, which is fulfilling one of their most cherished goals.

Most of their clothing is made by Amish women. These days they may use more modern synthetic fabrics than in the past. Clothing comes in different styles; some are designed for church and special events such as marriages and funerals, others for going out visiting or into town, and finally, some are especially durable, made for hard work. Each community's Ordnung will lay out rules regarding acceptable clothing, detailing the width of hat brims and length of women's dresses, for example. These are reviewed once or twice a year at meetings held before the communion services. Jewelry is not permitted, except in some communities in which copper rings and bracelets are allowed for people living with arthritis.

Women generally wear their long hair up in buns, braided or unbraided, parted in the middle; they do not cut their hair or shave. After marriage, men typically let their beards grow long but do not grow mustaches (they see an association between mustaches and the military). Their hair is often shaped in bowl cuts.

Women

Women generally wear plain, non-patterned, long-sleeved frock-style dresses with solid, muted colors accompanied with an apron (communities differ on apron color; in some, unmarried women wear black aprons until their wedding day, when they switch to white; in others, women wear white at home and if unmarried, black or purple if married or for church; some prefer white aprons and prayer caps for church; white aprons and prayer caps are always worn on the bride's wedding day and are saved for the woman's funeral), a black (sometimes white or colored if unmarried or younger) triangular cape is pinned into the apron, a prayer cap (in most cases white if baptized, black if not), a bonnet (usually white if unmarried, dark if married; these are generally worn when the woman is going out in public; a wagon bonnet extends on both sides to the shoulders; a poke bonnet with its deep brim conceals the wearer's profile; heavy bonnets may be worn in winter), black stockings and black lace-up shoes or boots. In winter, women may wear woolen cloaks or sweaters to keep warm, but usually not inside whatever house is holding the church service. Often they use straight pins, hooks and eyes, or snaps to fasten their clothing rather than buttons or zippers, especially for dress clothing. Prayer coverings can be made of different materials such as linen or organdy cotton and may be starched into stiff caps or left as softer caps. The prayer cap, of course, symbolizes the wife's subjugation to not only God but also to her husband. Some prayer caps have tie strings, and some do not. Those of the more conservative communities generally do.

Men

Men often wear blue denim for farm work but normally choose dark (usually black) broad-fall trousers with black suspenders (no belts), dark vests and plain, long-sleeved shirts (often white or light blue), sometimes with buttons (buttons and zippers are one of those gray areas; some do, some don't use them, according to the rules set out by the district's Ordnung; Old Order Amish men are likely to wear dress pants with pins or hooks and eyes rather than buttons or zippers; work clothing is more likely to sport buttons for practical purposes). They may wear straight-cut, lapel-less suit jackets fastened with hooks and eyes, depending on the weather.

Most wear black felt (winter) or straw (summer) broad-brimmed hats. The wider the hat brim and the lower the crown, the more conservative the community is. Black socks and black lace-up shoes adorn their feet. Married men sport beards but not mustaches; unmarried men are clean-shaven. The more conservative groups wear the bushier beards.

Children

Children's clothing is much the same as that of their parents but may be more expressive. Girls can wear colorful bonnets and capes until their teen years, when they usually switch to white or black (depending on the district's tradition) to indicate their unmarried (available) status. Girls as young as four years old begin wearing the traditional prayer cap and often have their hair braided rather than in a straight bun. They may wear pinafores. Small children may go around barefooted in spring, summer and fall.

Appliances, Tools and Equipment

Technology in the home

One question that was a real stumper for me when writing my first Amish novel was how these people powered kitchen appliances. I wanted to make sure I got this right so that I didn't look foolish. Electricity is forbidden in the Old Order Amish home (except in very rare circumstances when required for health reasons, such as to power oxygen equipment), so do they forgo all modern appliances and stick with iceboxes and wood cookstoves, or do they have another method? As it turns out, they have many different methods.

Once again, it is important to remember that they avoid technology not because they view it as inherently evil. It is true that technology is a direct connection to the rapidly progressing secular world that they dread. At one time, much of the technology they hold onto was the norm. But the world has zoomed ahead while they have by and large stayed behind. The Amish fear that unlimited usage of modern technology will undermine that close interdependence that is key to their way of life. They do not see hard work as an inconvenience but a necessity to hold families together. They also see us Moderns as using technology to make ourselves look better and more important than others, to indulge in one-upmanship against our neighbors, a pride-filled approach that contradicts the humble attitude they hold dear.

Rather than rejecting technology, the Amish use it cautiously and selectively, ensuring that it does not erode their traditional way of life.

So how do they power appliances and tools? Each community will differ, depending on the rules set down by its Ordnung. But what follows are some different options. As you read along, you will be amazed at how many different ways there are to accomplish the same goal without electricity. Electricity is handy (though in some places, costly), but with a little creativity, anyone can do without it. The Amish show us how.

First of all, how do they heat their homes? Some use woodstoves. If they have woodlots, this is an inexpensive way to keep their homes warm. Some may use coal stoves. Often wood or coal stoves are located in the basement. If on the first floor, they may double up as cooking stoves with top ovens installed. Or the cooking stove may do double duty as a heating stove, as they produce lots of heat. Other families use gas heaters, propane or natural. Their gas lanterns used for lighting also produce heat.

Do they pump water, or draw it up in a bucket from a well? Most of them pump water from dug wells. The most basic methods include hand pumps, but they may attach small engines to water pumps or use hydraulic pumps. Bathwater may be heated by gas water heaters, though some ultra-conservative homes may still use big copper kettles.

Although they shun electricity provided through the grid, they may use electricity in other forms. Batteries, such as 12-volt typically used in cars out in the world, are employed to power up small motors and buggy lanterns. Diesel or gas generators power electric equipment of various types for various uses. Generators are customarily used to run large workshop equipment, such as welders. Amish will use converters if required (for example, 12V to 110V). They use small internal combustible engines to saw wood, grind feed, pump water and power washing machines. Most use gasoline-powered lawnmowers, weed-eaters, chainsaws to keep their yards trim.

Lamps inside homes burn naphtha oil, kerosene or pressurized gas. They may use oil lamps for lighting, but most have switched to gas lanterns or battery-operated lamps. Lighting strictly by candle is uncommon except in ultra-conservative homes. Some homes are equipped with large gas lamps that roll to wherever they are needed in the main living areas.

Pneumatic-air and hydraulic-powered motors may be used for washing machines, sewing machines or food mixers. Propane gas or kerosene often fuels refrigerators and stoves. A few ultraconservatives still stick to iceboxes. Laundry is hung out (usually on Mondays after the weekend), so clothes are dried by wind power! A dishwasher would be hard to find in an Amish home; washing and drying dishes is a family event.

Many Amish are embracing renewable energy such as wind power (windmills or small turbines) and solar energy.

When an Amish family purchases a home that previously housed Moderns, they are usually allowed a grace period (six months to a year) during which they can use electricity while adapting the house over to conform to the particular requirements of their Ordnung.

Technology in businesses and on the farm

Electricity may be permitted in some businesses under some circumstances, especially if the Amish businessman is renting the space from an Englisher. Computers, telephones and cell phones are permitted in a few Amish businesses that must use them to carry on their operations effectively. Many woodworking tools in Amish shops are powered by hydraulic and pneumatic power run on diesel compressors.

Farm equipment involves a real balancing act for the Amish. They need it to be able to compete but must find the balance between lagging so far behind the times that they waste their resources to being so progressive that they begin to eliminate the need for manpower, replacing it with labor-saving technology (forcing their young men to seek employment in other occupations, such as non-Amish factories), or push their available resources to the brink, requiring the purchase of more and more farmland to justify the cost of their farm technology. The solution has been to set limits on the use of technology, all outlined in each district's Ordnung.

Field farm equipment is universally horse-drawn: plows, mowers, cultivators, harrows, hay balers. The Amish are adept at adapting modern farm equipment to become compatible with horses. They have struggled with the need to be competitive (not with each other but with non-Amish farmers), as mentioned earlier, while upholding Amish values, such as providing employment for their own and not amassing acreage (which is in very short supply in traditional Amish regions, making it difficult for young families to continue the farming tradition and live close to their families simultaneously).

And tractors, if they are owned, are stationed inside the barn to power other equipment: pumping liquid manure, powering ventilating equipment, operating feed grinders and energizing silage blowers. Many Ordnungs legislate that tractors be equipped with steel wheels rather than the more functional rubber tires so that they don't become used as automobile replacements! Although they are generally stationed inside barns, they can be used to pull equipment from place to place.

Solar-powered electric livestock fences are acceptable in many communities. Cows are often milked these days with vacuum machines (rather than by hand), and the milk is stored in bulk cooling tanks.

A few Amish farms are organic, but most are not. Organic farming is not stressed in most Amish communities as it is in some non-Amish regions. Many Amish farms are specialized, geared for a specific market.

Communication, Gadgets and Transportation

Telephone

Owning a telephone inside the home is generally forbidden. It is a direct connection to the outside world and may discourage those highly valued face-to-face interactions. A ringing telephone is viewed as an intrusion into the personal lives of Amish citizens. Some Amish families offer shared phone shanties, usually at the end of a driveway, from which neighbors can make and/or receive calls, especially in emergencies. Generally, they are used for making calls.

Some Amish are allowed phones in their businesses to be able to interact with suppliers and customers. Often there are strict rules about when and how the telephone can be used in the district's Ordnung. Amish business owners also employ cell phones and voicemail services.

Computer

Personal home computers, especially with Internet access, are not permitted, but Amish can and do use computers in their workplaces. Most can have a website for their own small business, but it must be designed and hosted by a non-Amish intermediary.

Camera

Photo-taking is banned, as the Amish view it as possibly breaking the Biblical injunction against making graven images in the second of the Ten Commandments (Exodus 20:4). Close-up photos in which the subjects can be recognized are especially forbidden. Tourists love to photograph the Amish, though, when in Amish country. Posing for photos is forbidden for baptized church members, but unbaptized children may not be disciplined if they give in. Being caught in long-distance photos for which the Amish adult has not given consent is not grounds for discipline.

Transportation

Nothing represents freedom quite as much to the North American as those four wheels on his or her automobile. They have the power to take a person just about wherever he or she wishes to go. This liberty represents everything the Amish reject: the freedom to ride the roads, to get away from it all. The Amish value responsibility to family and community. They are firmly rooted in their homes.

The horse is as symbolic for the Amish as the car is for the average North American. The horse represents being patient, following tradition, setting limits. The horse and buggy mode of transport keeps communities tight-knit, with members dependent on each other. The maximum distance a horse pulling a carriage buggy can travel is about 25 miles, without taking a long rest. The maximum speed the horse can muster is about 10 mph. So, by being dependent on their horses for travel, the Amish ensure that most of their activities take place close to home. However, as fundamental as the horse and buggy are to the Amish way of life, horseback riding is much less common, seen more as a sport than a valid means of transportation.

Horses, too, differ, depending on their roles. The Amish own sleek driving horses, sometimes purchased from racetracks, as well as the stockier workhorses to pull farm equipment.

Today buggies look much the same as their precursors but may be made of fiberglass with thermopane windows. Many are equipped with orange "slow-moving" triangular reflector safety signs to adhere to local regulations.

Although they do not own cars, Amish will ride in Englishers' cars or hire drivers, if need be, perhaps to go to social events in other Amish districts or for monthly shopping excursions out of town. They will also ride on public transportation, such as trains or buses, which cannot enhance the rider's status (car ownership is seen as bringing the risk of pride of ownership). Amish businessmen use non-Amish vehicles to transport goods to customers, or materials and inventory from suppliers.

Often when a boy turns 16, his parents will buy him a small buggy with a horse. He may use this for courting his wife-to-be. An open buggy is often called a courting buggy. It is much smaller than the standard enclosed carriage with bench seats, which is the family buggy that can hold up to six people (or more if they are squeezed in). These usually have window glass and sliding side doors and may be equipped with a rumble seat. Wives sit on the left of their husbands, again a sign of subjugation. Today, some buggies are equipped with advanced safety features such as battery-operated head and rear lights, turn signals, flashing lights (though some conservative groups still use gas or kerosene lanterns) and caution signs. We tend to think of buggies being black, but some carriages are white or yellow, depending on the community's traditions.

Other useful Amish vehicles employed in farm and other work situations include the spring wagon, used for transporting heavy objects; the market wagon, used to bring goods to farm markets; the compact farm wagon, light enough for a small horse to pull and employed in a variety of ways; and the handy two-wheeled cart.

Some communities acknowledge their Amish population by posting yellow caution signs displaying the horse and buggy symbol on main roads. They may have hitching posts along the main shopping street in town.

Bicycles, non-motorized scooters and roller blades are permitted in some communities, but not others. If you are an author, you have the authority to allow such pastimes in your Amish community if doing so enhances your story.

Amish Language

Amish speak a Germanic language at home, popularly called Pennsylvania Dutch. Pennsylvania German is a more appropriate name for the language as the expression Pennsylvania Dutch originated from Pennsylvania Deutsch, and Deutsch means German. Children from more conservative homes learn English for the first time at school. At church, they speak High German along with Pennsylvania Dutch.

If you are writing fiction, it is recommended that a few Pennsylvania Dutch words be sprinkled into an Amish novel. Don't overdo this, or, besides driving your spell check feature crazy, the book will become incomprehensible to those not familiar with Pennsylvania Dutch (the large majority of your readership). You can include a glossary at the end of your book that provides the translations of the Pennsylvania Dutch words you used.

What follows is by no means a complete Pennsylvania Dutch dictionary. Those are available online. But I've included a few words and expressions to get you started.

As a rule, the Amish address each other by their first names rather than using titles.

As you've gathered from reading this book, we non-Amish are called Englishers (sometimes spelled Englischers). Or Moderns.

What are some other commonly used Pennsylvania Dutch words, phrases, expressions? To complicate things, Pennsylvania Dutch spellings vary slightly from region to region, so try to be consistent in using your particular dictionary source's spellings.

A few word examples:

Amisch (Amish), niedrich (humble), deheem (at home), waegli (buggy).

Jah (yes), nee (no), ach (oh), danka (thank you), gut (good), wunderbaar (wonderful).

Gott (God), mann (man), mansleit (men folk).

Biewel (the Bible), der Herr (Lord), breddicher (minister), kurich (church), Nachtmol (Lord's Supper), daaf (baptism), lied (song), karichelied (hymn), Sunndaag (Sunday).

Haus (house), scheier (barn), kich (kitchen), bauereie (farm).

Family relationships: shtamm (family), fraa (wife), vadder (father), daed (dad), mudder (mother), maemm (mom), bruder (brother), shveshtah (sister), buwe (son), dochtah (daughter), grossdaddi and grossmammi (grandfather and grandmother), maedel (girl), kinner (children) or kinder (kids) or kins-kind (grandchildren), bobli (baby), onkel (uncle), ant (aunt).

Colors: weiss (white), brau (brown), bloo (blue), dunkel (dark).

Popular food and drink: kaffe (coffee), brot (bread), millich (milk), fleesch (meat), gaardesach (vegetables), grumbeer (potato). Esa! (Eat!) as a command is popular.

Clothing: kapp (prayer cap), hut (hat), gaellesse (suspenders).

Activities: schaffe (work), schlof (sleep).

Animals: gaul (horse), bussli (kitten), kuh (cow), hinkel (chicken).

Nature: bliehe (flower), ern (harvest), erd (earth), baam (tree), busch (woods).

And, finally, for those romance writers: lieb (love), hochzich (wedding).

There are, of course, many others you can choose, depending on your storyline.

Using full Pennsylvania Dutch expressions is likely to confuse readers. Expressions such as "sie scheie sich vun haddiArewat" ("they shrink from hard work") and "er harricht gut, awwer er foligt schlecht" ("he hears well, but obeys poorly") will require complete translations in English so may not enhance your story. "Gott segen eich" ("God bless you") or "guten nacht" ("good night") could be used in dialogue. "Wie bischt du" ("How are you?") may be best left out.

If you do meet an Amish individual, and he or she asks, "Kannscht du Pennsilfaanisch Deitsch schwetzer?", you may realize that he or she is asking you if you speak Pennsylvania Dutch. Your best bet may be to politely shake your head "no" and continue your conversation in English.

Common Amish Names, First and Last, for Fiction Writers

You have sat down to write your Amish novel. A beautiful plot has unfolded in your mind, and you are anxious to get it down on paper (or more likely computer drive) as quickly as possible before you lose it. But right away, you are faced with a problem that is slowing you down and ruining your momentum. What to name your characters? It's important to give especially your heroine and hero names used in Amish communities and to which your readers will be drawn. So what to choose so that you can get on with the plot development?

For Amish fiction, sticking with Biblical first names is a good option, though if the Biblical character has a poor reputation (such as Nimrod or Bathsheba), you might want to keep looking. You will find more male than female names in the Bible, and there's a good chance more of your main characters will be female than male. Especially in romance fiction, the heroine is often the main character from whose perspective the book is written. What female name can you choose that hasn't been used a thousand times before? Here are a few possibilities. And, yes, they've likely been used a thousand times before. But don't worry about that. Your story will be different in the ways that count.

Female first names (some are Biblical) that could be used in Amish fiction: Abigail, Ada, Angela, Anna, Barbara, Bernice, Bethany, Beulah, Candace, Carmel, Charity, Chloe, Claudia, Cornelia, Deborah, Delilah (pretty but somewhat negative associations), Dinah, Dorothy, Eden, Edna, Elizabeth, Emma, Esther, Eunice, Eva or Eve, Faith, Gloria, Grace, Hannah, Honey, Hope, Hosanna, Irene, Jedidiah, Jemimah, Joanna, Joy, Judith, Julia, Katharine, Keturah, Leah, Lillian or Lily, Lois, Lydia, Martha, Mary, Mercy, Micah, Miriam, Myra, Nancy, Naomi, Nicole, Phoebe, Priscilla, Rachel, Rebecca, Ruth, Salome, Sarah, Sharon, Shiloh, Sophia, Susan, Tabitha, Tamar or Tamara, Theodora, Victoria, Zipporah.

Amish or Bible-related male first names that could be chosen: Aaron, Abel, Abner, Abraham, Adam, Albert, Alexander, Amos, Andrew, Barnabas, Benjamin, Cain, Christian, Clement, Cornelius, Cyrus, Daniel or Dan, David, Ebenezer, Eli, Elijah, Elisha, Elmo, Emmanuel, Ethan, Ezekiel, Ezra, Felix, Gabriel, Gideon, Hezekiah, Isaac, Isaiah, Ishmael, Israel, Jacob, James, Jared, Jason, Jedidiah, Jeremiah, Jesse, Jethro, Joel, John, Jonah, Jordan, Joseph, Joshua, Josiah, Jude, Laban, Lazarus, Levi, Lloyd, Luke, Manasseh, Mark, Marvin, Matthew, Michael, Moses, Nathan or Nathaniel, Nicholas, Noah, Paul, Peter, Philip, Reuben, Roy, Rufus, Samuel, Saul, Seth, Simon, Solomon, Stephen, Thaddeus, Thomas, Timothy, Titus, Tobias, Zachary.

Your choice of Amish surnames is limited. If you read Amish fiction, you will see the same last names pop up again and again. There is no getting around this. After all, today's Amish are descendants of a relatively small number of European immigrants. Some possible choices: Albrecht, Bawell, Beiler, Bontrager, Brandenberger, Fisher, Gascho, Gingerich, Graber, Hershberger, Hochstellar, Jantzi, King, Lapp, Lee, Mast, Miller, Neuenschwander, Ropp, Schlabach, Schmucker, Schrock, Schwartz, Stoltzfus, Troyer, Weaver, Yoder, Zook.

Conclusion

So, are you ready to write that Amish novel that is begging to be written?! Or are you venturing into a nonfiction book or report about these fascinating people? If you still don't feel confident, you may want to research more before starting, and there are other resources available in printed form and on the Web. If you are fortunate enough to live close to a district, it would be a great idea to pay them a visit and learn firsthand. Just leave your camera or tablet at home if you don't want to get off to a bad start. The information in this book should help you launch into your writing with the confidence that comes with the backing of extensive research. As your work evolves, you may want to research specific aspects of their lifestyle, such as Amish wedding recipes.

Reading good Amish fiction and nonfiction is also recommended. Just be careful to compare the text against sound facts to ensure the writer has done his or her research so that you aren't misled!

Do you feel you don't agree with the Amish on some important points, that you can't go along with all of their beliefs and practices? Don't dwell on it. Your role as a writer is to bring your subjects to life as genuine Amish people, with beliefs and practices that are common to the group. There is some latitude as districts vary significantly on some aspects, such as apron color and buggy lighting, but there are also fundamental philosophies that tie them together. If you are writing fiction, it's cool for your characters to struggle with traditional Amish beliefs, but it's not cool for you to whitewash your district and turn them into something the Amish are not. One of the main complaints of Amish readers is that non-Amish novelists, often evangelical Christians eager to impart the salvation message, transform their Amish characters into people who have completely different guiding life principles than mainstream Amish.

If you have found the information in this book useful, if you feel it will save you time in your own research, please take a moment to leave a review. Doing so will help other writers, and those who are simply interested in learning more about the Amish, find this book amidst the large crowds on Amazon and other book-publishing marketplaces.

As stated in the introduction, feedback regarding this book would be highly valued and can be sent to *dgailauthor@gmail.com*.

Thanks very much for purchasing this book.

About the Author

D. Gail and D. Gail Miller are pennames. Pennames are more commonly used by ghostwriters stepping out of the closet, for obvious reasons. I began writing fiction back in the 1970s when still in university. Fiction-writing was so compelling that my studies suffered. My early attempts revolved around favorite rock stars but took a 360-degree turn in the mid-1980s following my born-again conversion to Christianity. Afterward, I wrote numerous Christian-based novels and short stories, mainly for youth, interspersed with editing jobs.

After taking a break from writing because of the demands of 80 hours a week of "paid" employment, I recently returned to writing and editing as a freelancer and have worked under contract. However, current self-publishing opportunities have proved too tempting, and mainly independent writing alongside contract editing and editorial services provided to other indie writers comprise my new career blueprint.

Although I cannot (under contract) reference my Amish ghostwritten fiction, I have self-published a few Amish novels under my D. Gail Miller penname, such as *The Amish Old House Mysteries* series available on Amazon: (https://www.amazon.com/Amish-Old-House-Mysteries-Book/dp/B075D8NFRB/ref=sr_1_11?_encoding=UTF8&dchild=1&qid=1614783011&refinements=p_27%3AD.+Gail+Miller&s=digital-text&sr=1-11)

www.ingramcontent.com/pod-product-compliance
Lightning Source LLC
Chambersburg PA
CBHW060715030426
42337CB00017B/2876